THE PAINTED SWAGMAN

This book is dedicated, in gratitude and admiration, to our early pioneers of all origins; and to our modern pioneers who continue to Advance Australia.

Certain real persons and events from Australia's colourful past are mentioned in this book. They are faithfully reported from the historical record.

The fictional characters are entirely imaginary and are not intended to portray any real persons, living or deceased. Especially, their invented natures bear no resemblance to those of the Australian men, women and children who modelled for them in the paintings.

In the text, the units of measurement contemporary to the period of the story have been used:

There are twelve pence to the shilling,
twenty shillings to the pound; and
one pound is equivalent to two dollars.
One mile approximates 1.6 kilometres.
One acre approximates 0.4 hectares.

THE PAINTED SWAGMAN

A TRIBUTE TO
"Waltzing Matilda"

ORIGINAL STORY and PAINTINGS by DOROTHY GAUVIN

HERITAGE GALLERY PRINTING

HERITAGE GALLERY PRINTING

First published in Australia in 1995 by
Heritage Gallery Printing (BN 552 8677)
10 Crest Close, Bayview Heights, Cairns
Queensland 4870, Australia

Distributed in Australia by
Herron Books
91 Main Street, Kangaroo Point, Brisbane
Queensland 4169, Australia

National Library of Australia
Cataloguing-in-Publication data:

Gauvin, Dorothy
  The painted swagman

  ISBN 0 646 22370 4

  I Waltzing Matilda II Title

Cover painting by Dorothy Gauvin

Typeset in Australia by DOCUPRO, Sydney
Printed in Australia by McPhersons Printing Group

This book produced entirely in Australia

CONTENTS

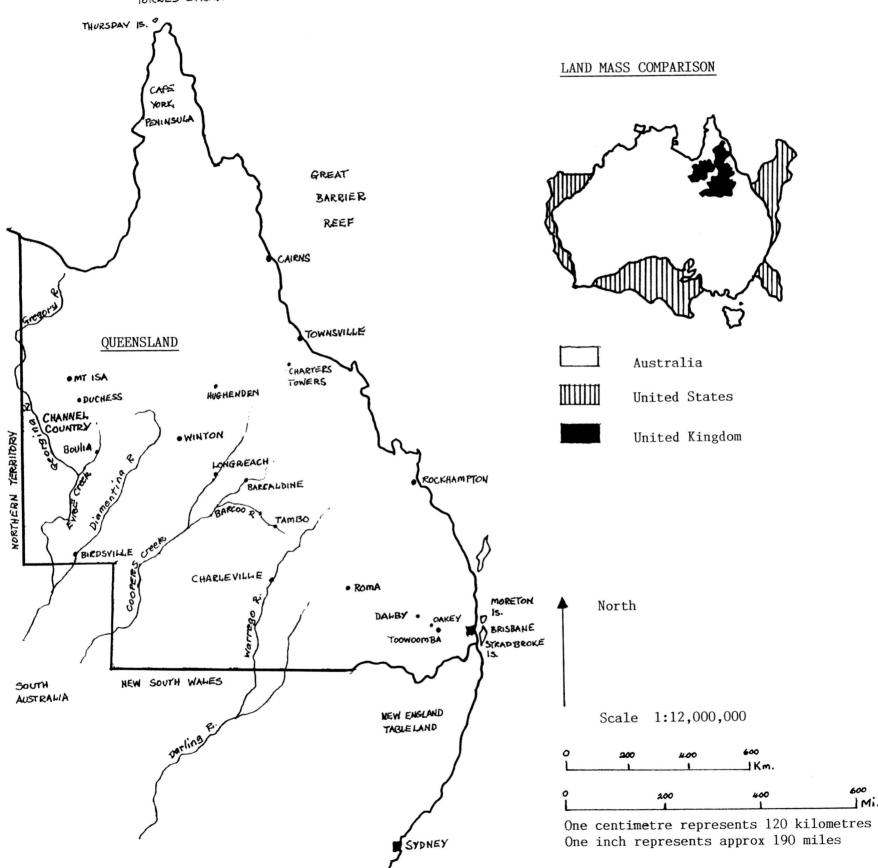

TORRES STRAIT

THURSDAY IS.

CAPE
YORK
PENINSULA

GREAT

BARRIER

REEF

CAIRNS

Gregory R.

QUEENSLAND

TOWNSVILLE

CHARTERS
TOWERS

MT ISA

DUCHESS

HUGHENDEN

CHANNEL
COUNTRY

Georgina R.

Eyre Creek

Diamentina R.

WINTON

Boulia

LONGREACH

BARCALDINE

ROCKHAMPTON

NORTHERN TERRITORY

Barcoo R.

TAMBO

Coopers Creek

BIRDSVILLE

CHARLEVILLE

ROMA

MORETON
IS.

Warrego R.

DALBY

OAKEY

BRISBANE

TOOWOOMBA

STRADBROKE
IS.

SOUTH
AUSTRALIA

NEW SOUTH WALES

NEW ENGLAND
TABLELAND

Darling R.

SYDNEY

LAND MASS COMPARISON

Australia

United States

United Kingdom

North

Scale   1:12,000,000

0   200   400   600
                                        Km.

0   200   400   600
                                        Mi.

One centimetre represents 120 kilometres
One inch represents approx 190 miles

Australia is famous as a land whose people are addicted to nicknames and the country has borne a fair share of these. The very first was coined by early European mapmakers who called it Terra Australis Incognito: The Unknown South Land. The Land Downunder, The Lucky Country, The Sunburnt Land; these are the names best known outside Australia. But to true-blue, fair-dinkum Aussies, the homeland is simply called Oz.

Nothing more magical awaited Dorothy and Toto, after their whirlwind trip from Kansas, than greets today's visitor to this actual Land of Oz.

When Captain Cook and his company invented the Australian tourism industry back in 1770, they were enchanted by giant 'mice' which bounded across the plains on overgrown hind legs; by cuddly 'bears' which curled sleepily in gumtrees and never drank a sip of water; by enormous kingfishers which cracked snakes as though they were stockwhips, all the time laughing and cackling like a maniacs' picnic. These kangaroos, koalas and kookaburras still delight travellers to The Timeless Land.

These, and many other animal oddities, are only the introduction to a range of fascinating contrasts which Australia presents. The undersea gardens of the Great Barrier Reef, above which float dreamlike tropical resort islands, are stunningly offset by the endless desert which fills most of the continent. In its Red Heart, the monolithic Uluru, or Ayer's Rock, puts on a magic lantern show of shifting colours each dawn and dusk.

The white-tiled 'sails' which roof Sydney's Opera House appear to billow in the breezes off the Harbour, while in outback Longreach, a futuristic reminder of the pioneers' tin sheds houses the magnificent Stockmen's Hall of Fame. But the most amazing statistic about Australia remains the tiny population which peoples this vast territory. A look at the map opposite will show you some comparisons which graphically illustrate the situation.

With a population of only 18 million, Australia's land mass is little less than that of the continental United States of America; the United Kingdom of Great Britain could be squeezed into Cape York, that 'pointy bit' at the top of Queensland. The state of Queensland occupies one-fifth of Australia's land mass, but the American state of Texas could fit within its borders two-and-a-half times.

The truest treasure of any country lies in its people, and the Australians' genius for reasonableness — for being ever willing to 'give the other bloke a fair go' — has created a multicultural society widely regarded as surprisingly stable and harmonious amid the troubled nations of our shared planet.

Such a happy state of affairs does not come about by accident. The answer can be found in the nature of ordinary Australians, moulded by the demands of an excessively challenging environment, and the colourful history which formed the national character.

One hundred years ago exactly, the world

suffered a global economic crisis which has recently been mirrored with stunning exactitude. In both cases, Australia was among the first to shiver in the icy winds of recession.

Previously unimaginable sights would have shocked you, had you walked through Australian cities of the 1890s. Beggars appeared on street corners; homeless families camped overnight in the city parks; unemployed men languished in ever-lengthening queues for non-existent jobs. As the disaster escalated, those with enough get-up-and-go left the despair of the cities and flocked to sunny Queensland where the great wheat farms and sheep and cattle runs held out hope for casual work.

These men, and a very few intrepid women, rolled their swags and went Bush. But in Queensland they ran into the violent labour struggle now known as The Shearers' War which ended in late 1894.

Ten thousand armed rebel shearers and unionists confronted the police and the defence force soon to become famous as The Light Horse. Pitched battles were fought in which thousands of rounds of ammunition were exchanged, 'scab' labourers forcibly abducted into strike camps, and a king's ransom in woolsheds and baled fleeces destroyed by arson.

Yet, in the bloody annals of civil warfare, this one is unique in claiming not a single life in combat during the Queensland campaign. The only death was by a mysterious suicide.

This book will take you on a journey back to a legendary period that had immense effect on the development of a national identity and which still resonates in the political and social life of all Australians.

Our adventure begins in Sydney during the wintry weather of May 1893. In the streets, cable trams jostle for space with the horse-drawn omnibuses and hansom cabs. Outside the locked doors of one of the many failed banks, two young optimists set up business as buskers, while anxious men queue beneath a Help Wanted sign.

When only one worker is taken on, the others fall to discussing the last resort option known as 'following the wallaby track'. What it means is tramping the back country roads in search of casual work for cash to send back in support of families left behind.

Bill Conlan is one who decides on this course of action. We watch as he rolls his swag which, for reasons lost to time, is called 'Matilda', or else known as a 'bluey' for the blankets which make up its bulk.

On the Track, many travellers prefer to give only their first name or a nickname and personal questions are rarely encouraged. But Bill has no reason to hide his identity. He will be our guide on a journey during which we will meet many of the off-beat characters of the Outback. With Bill, we will travel through changing landscapes and dramatic shifts in social attitudes as the 19th Century draws to a close.

The Australian swag was born of Australia and no other land – of the great lone land of magnificent distances and bright heat; the land of self-reliance, and never-give-in, and help-your-mate. the grave of many of the world's tragedies and comedies — royal and otherwise. The land where a man out of employment might shoulder his swag in Adelaide and take the track, and years later walk into a hut on the Gulf, or never be heard of any more, or a body be found in the bush and buried by the mounted police, or never found and never buried — what does it matter?

Travelling with the swag in Australia is variously and picturesquely described as "humping bluey", "walking Matilda", "humping Matilda", "humping your drum", "being on the wallaby", "jabbing trotters", and "tea and sugar burglaring", but most travelling shearers now call themselves trav'lers, and say simply "on the track", or "carrying swag".

The Australian swag has held in its core letters and papers in all languages, the honour of great houses, and more than one national secret, papers that would send well-known and highly-respected men to jail, and proofs of the innocence of men going mad in prisons, life tragedies and comedies, fortunes and papers that secured titles and fortunes, and the last pence of lost fortunes, life secrets, portraits of mothers and dead loves, pictures of fair women, heart-breaking old letters written long ago by vanished hands, and the pencilled manuscript of more than one book which will be famous yet.

Henry Lawson (1901)

CHAPTER ONE

May 1893, Sydney

All the millionaires were gone from Sydney's streets. Vanished were the entrepreneurs who had fashioned outrageous fortunes from the flash-fire of land and building speculation which engulfed the city during the 'Eighties. Some had crumpled into bankruptcy. Others had decamped abroad with funds creamed from their unlucky shareholders. Their extravagant lifestyles, which had enlivened the Harbour City and glittered from the pages of every newspaper for the past decade, had faded away with them.

The legitimate wealthy had built their fortunes slowly in enterprises which generated jobs and prosperity within Australia. Precious few of them were left. Cutting costs where they could, they held on in businesses and farm properties, watching their interest payments soar while the prices for their products plummeted. With all their anxieties, they were still better off than the tens of thousands thrown into unemployment. In common decency, most now refrained from any public display of their remaining wealth.

Still, each day, the city throbbed with traffic. Its hilly roadways rattled with horse-drawn omnibuses bringing shoppers from the new suburbs. Cable trams plied the inner city streets, filled with commuters who had arrived by ferry from across the Harbour. From the heart of the city, whistle blasts signalled the movement of trains at Redfern Station. In from the rural areas they came laden with produce for the city's markets; with coal for its factories' furnaces; with wool clips and frozen beef for its export trade.

Teams of stolid clydesdales transported loads from the wool stores and breweries and warehouses along to Circular Quay where steamships waited to carry their cargoes the immense length of the Australian coastline or across the oceans to markets in London and New York. Like most of the crowd, Bill Conlan tried not to stare at the dejected lines of people queuing for government relief rations. He could only feel grateful that his job at the chemist shop was still secure, providing for Tess and their little son Billy.

DRAWING·IN·PROGRESS

THE PAINTED SWAGMAN

11

His height gave Bill a clear view over the heads of most in the crowd. Although he was in a hurry this morning, his long stride faltered as he caught sight of some newcomers on Beggars' Corner. Two boys, obviously brothers; they had the same eyes, same hair, same skinny build. Barefoot and blue-legged in the morning chill, they sat tailor-fashion on the wide steps of a bankrupt banking house.

At their feet was propped a sign lettered in a careful, childish hand: 'Thank You'. That sign had captured Bill's attention. The optimism it implied did not belong on Beggars' Corner. Neither did these boys. Set up as street musicians, they looked ready to give value for anything dropped into the man-sized hat upturned beside them.

The slowing of Bill's steps was enough to galvanise them into action. The older boy had his mouth organ squeaking away even as he scrambled to his feet. He danced a jig of more energy than grace while his brother piped on a battered penny whistle. Bill just recognised the tune they were mangling as the old convict sea shanty 'Bound for Botany Bay'. Digging into his pocket, he fished out the coins he had saved by walking to work instead of taking the tram.

Uncomfortably aware of how little difference it could make to the situation of these kids, he added his small donation to the few coppers already collected in their hat. By that evening, Bill's own situation was thrown into chaos when the chemist sadly announced that he was now forced to close down.

Tess' careful management had provided a modest savings account which promised Bill a couple of months' grace in which to look for another position but he knew the path ahead of him was all uphill. With few skills and little enough education provided by the orphanage in which he had been raised, Bill knew his chances in a desperately over-supplied labour market were very slim. His only assets were a strong back and a fierce determination not to be dependent on handouts.

DRAWING-IN-PROGRESS

THE PAINTED SWAGMAN

A financial crisis of global proportions had erupted during the November of 1890 when Argentina defaulted on bond payments to Baring Brothers, the great merchant bankers of England. The London stock exchange was riddled with panic which soon infected Australia.

Between August 1891 and the first days of May 1893, sixteen major banks and about fifty building societies closed their doors in a banking dilemma which began in Tasmania, escalated in Victoria and then spread throughout the nation.

At the time, the typical wage for an ordinary labouring man was sixty pence per day; for a female factory outworker it was ten pence per day. But as one businessman after another was forced to close his doors and walk away, any capital he had left locked up in the failed banks, jobs disappeared with him.

In some places, riots broke out when poverty-stricken tenants were turned out into the streets. Soon the city parks became camping grounds at night for the homeless, some taking up residence in the caves which pitted the cliffs facing the sea.

As the winter bit harder, many jobless men and a few intrepid women rolled whatever remained of their possessions into a swag of blankets covered in canvas. This would be their only shelter as they tramped the bush tracks in hopes of finding some better way of life.

Many died of exposure and were buried where they dropped; uncounted others simply vanished. Their only testimonial was to come with the writings of Bush balladists such as Henry Lawson and 'Banjo' Paterson.

During the exodus of unemployed men from the despair of the cities, about one hundred thousand of them flocked into Queensland where the sprawling wheat farms and woolsheds offered a chance for casual work. Bill began to prepare himself and Tess for the possibility that he might have to join that band of travellers.

DRAWING·IN·PROGRESS

THE PAINTED SWAGMAN

15

In a month of fruitless job-hunting, Bill heard a lot about the option known as 'following the wallaby track'. What it meant was walking the country roads, looking for odd jobs on the farms and in the townships. At the worst, a dole of rations could be collected from the country police stations, though it was said the police were not keen on having a travelling man stay in their towns for more than one night.

Of the men in the queues that Bill daily haunted, he noticed that the fellows most taken with the idea of going on the road were those already homeless and without families. Others were tired of the endless struggle and eager to leave behind the constant reminders of their failure to provide for what families they had. It seemed to Bill that the fellows who talked the loudest knew little of what was entailed.

Old hands who had tramped the back roads during the last Depression, back in the 'Sixties, held no illusions that to go 'waltzing with Matilda' was any romantic adventure. When such a man talked on the subject, Bill paid close attention for there were few blokes in the queue with any real experience of the Bush.

In the most urbanised nation on Earth, most were city born and bred or, like himself, had come in from the rural towns at an early age. Though colourful theories abounded, nobody really knew how the phrase had originated, but Bill hoped 'waltzing Matilda' was an option he would not be forced to take. He was spared this uncertainty when he was signed on with a gang of general hands to work the season at a sheep station in far-off Queensland.

Bill felt anything was better than the continuing round of rejections in the city work queues and Tess tearfully agreed. They had a harder time convincing little Billy that where his dad was going was only for the working men and that he was relied on to stay home and take care of his mother. With a violent send-off by unionists protesting the use of 'scab' labour to break the renewed strikes by shearers in Queensland, Bill's train steamed out of Sydney, headed for the sheep country.

DRAWING·IN·PROGRESS

THE PAINTED SWAGMAN

On the train journey to Queensland, Bill began to sense the vastness of the land he had always called Home, without experiencing more than a pocket-sized portion of it. Though he had carefully added up the distance from Sydney to Toowoomba on the Darling Downs, those seven hundred miles had been only figures on a map. Now the long days of travel — and the even longer nights — fixed the distance in his mind as a physical reality.

Landed at Glenkillen Station, Bill and the other workers were astounded by the opulence of the bluestone homestead mansion and its landscaped gardens. They soon discovered this elegance did not extend to the accommodations for the seasonal labourers. The shearers' quarters were mean huts with only open doorways for ventilation. Seried bunks climbed the slab walls, their mildewed canvas bases bare of bedding or mattresses. In the dark interior, they found no other furniture but a rough table and rickety chairs on the antbed floor.

Like most city folk, Bill's impression of his country's rural landholders was coloured by the reports of them selected by newspaper columnists. The perception conveyed was of an idle, privileged club of people who floated through life on a sea of champagne, pursuing entertainments such as polo and fox-hunting which were incomprehensible to the ordinary folk whose labour had made them rich.

Having never yet crossed paths with one of the squatters of the western districts, who put in as long and hard a day as any of their men, Bill's view was only confirmed by the evident meanness of the absentee owner of this particular sheep station.

Glenkillen had been carved from the virgin Downs when convicts still toiled in chain gangs at the labour camps of Moreton Bay. His hard-working ancestors would have been deeply disappointed in the current young heir. Leaving the property to the dubious care of a manager he had imported from England, he spent most of the year touring the fashionable resorts of Europe and following the social whirl of London.

DRAWING-IN-PROGRESS

Bill and several other hands were told to doss down in the stables. They counted themselves luckier than the shearers — despite their prestige and much higher pay — for the horses here were better housed than the men. At night, the soft snufflings of the horses became a lullaby which, after his day of hard labour, sent Bill quickly into a sleep without dreams. Each day, he learned something new about sheep handling.

Due to the disruptions caused by continuing strike action, shearing was now way behind on Glenkillen. Further delays grew from the manager's arrogant insistence that the flocks be scoured before shearing. The practice was outmoded, for as sheep runs gained access to the ports by rail, the extra freight costs of dirt embedded in the fleece became negligible. But on Glenkillen, Bill and the others stood all day, waist deep in the washpool, scrubbing resentful sheep with an evil-smelling mixture of ammonia and soap.

On this station, it was the boss shearer who made the decision as to whether the flock was dry enough for shearing. One morning, this man pronounced the sheep dry and Joseph Canning, the sensible and efficient overseer, nodded his agreement. Once inside the shed, Canning was boss of the board and he appointed each man to his station. Fourteen shearer's stands opened along one side of the building and most of them were taken up by the gang of 'Free' (non-union) blademen. Three thousand bleating animals were already

gathered in the holding pens inside the massive shed. Even if it should rain, these sheep would stay dry for shearing.

Bill noticed that every post of the inner holding pens was decorated with simple or fanciful designs; no doubt, they had been whittled there over the years by bored shearers waiting for the rain to stop. Within an hour of the start of shearing, the air was saturated with flying wisps of wool fibres and with the grunts of sweating men as they stooped to make the first sweeping cuts which would separate each animal from its fleece.

DRAWING·IN·PROGRESS

One by one, the sheep were grabbed from the pens, dragged to the stands and wrestled onto their broad backs where they lay placid and unprotesting as the blades flashed over their bodies. From time to time, the blades would pink a sheep, for the shearers were paid by the hundred shorn and so speed was more desirable than finesse. At the cry of 'Tar here!', Bill or one of the other rouseabouts would come running with the tarpot to staunch the animal's wound before the shearer released it, shoving it down a chute to join its bald mates in the yards outside.

As each day neared its close, a ripple of excitement ran through the ranks as they eyed the blackboard on which the shearers' names were posted. Each man's tally was daily entered alongside and at day's end, they waited eagerly to see who had rung the shed. The race for title of ringer had settled to a contest between two gun shearers who had often worked the western sheds and each of them consistently scored a tally of close to two hundred for the day. Whichever of them triumphed, this pair modestly shrugged it off, calling it nothing compared with what could be done by Jackie Howe.

The ringer called Barney reckoned he had been in the gang on that famous day, one year earlier, when the champion had broken the world record for hand shearing. Smoko was a welcome respite from the back-breaking work and the shearing gang stretched aching muscles and wiped off rivers of sweat before settling to the cook's offering of brownies and scalding tea, while a boy swept the board clean under the watchful eye of the overseer.

Some of the men present knew that if every blademan who claimed to have shorn alongside Jackie Howe on that fabled day was telling the truth, it must have been the most crowded shed in history. Still, everyone listened intently as Barney related the tale.

'Three hundred and twenty-one, Jackie shore. In seven hours, forty minutes. Could've been more but the blokes wouldn't let him go on. He'd broke the record, see. Enough's enough, we reckoned. Yer don't want a bloke gettin' too big fer his boots.'

DRAWING·IN·PROGRESS

"SMOKO IN THE WOOLSHED"

THE PAINTED SWAGMAN

—
23

When the season on Glenkillen ended, Bill tried his luck with the farmers of the district; and found that luck had deserted him. Medium or small, they had no work to offer. Most of them had left the daily running of the farms to the wives and children while they competed for the few cash jobs available.

These were to be found on the tobacco fields around Texas and Killarney, an area some described as 'the Virginia of Australia'. Some jobs were to be had in the vineyards of Middle Ridge where German planters had put three hundred and forty acres under grapes. But in three weeks, Bill scored only a few days' work and then decided his best course was to strike out for the provincial capital of Toowoomba.

On the first night of his trek towards that town, Bill camped beneath the stars. By the flickering light of his campfire, he started a long letter to Tess, setting out the plan he had conceived as he travelled through the farming regions. Looking back on that frustrating period, Bill considered it a turning point in his life for he believed it had shown him the means by which he might achieve his goal of independence and security.

During that journey around the farms, Bill had kept his eyes and ears wide open and had filled pages of his letter-pad with notes on what he had observed. Energised with hope when he learned of the government's 'Homesteader Plan' to populate this huge state by offering small holdings at cheap rates, he was convinced this was the answer. At sixpence per acre per year, with five years to pay it off, they could own a block freehold.

They would be self-sufficient. Never again would they be at the mercy of man-made disasters like this present Depression and all those which had preceded it. The one stumbling block was the starting capital needed. Bill calculated that to set up the venture properly, he and Tess needed a stake of ninety pounds; and he had no idea of how they would save that kind of money. But now he had a goal to work towards and he was determined to make the dream into a reality.

DRAWING·IN·PROGRESS

"THE HOMESTEADERS"

THE PAINTED SWAGMAN

CHAPTER THREE

October 1893, Toowoomba

At Toowoomba, the gardener's craft was raised to art. Bill walked along streets lined with camphor laurels and jacarandas, past house yards perfumed by flowers of every shade and shape. In the broad main street, hardly a thing moved. The shuttered shopfronts were no surprise, for as if he had needed a reminder that this was Sunday, the carolling of bells from a clutch of churches had rolled out to meet him as he neared the town.

The fluttering of a flag led Bill to the police station where the grossly fat sergeant on duty eyed him curiously while he explained that he was looking for work of any kind. Following the sergeant's directions, Bill made his way to a nearby blacksmith who, the policeman had assured him, was looking for an offsider and was sure to be at work regardless of its being Sunday.

The reason for this became clear soon after Bill presented himself to the smith. Otto Leibniz was a blocky man with the appearance of having been built out of house bricks. Great biceps bulged below the short sleeves of his woollen shirt and Bill noticed many small burn scars beneath the skin of his forearms. Inside the shop it was much cooler than he expected and his puzzled glance at the unlit forge was noted by the smith.

'It is Gott's holy day for most people here, Herr Conlan. I do not offend their Sabbath with belching smoke and noise. In turn, I ask them to respect my ways.'

A few days later, the smithy was visited by d'Arcy Malone, chief union organiser in the town. Politely, Bill endured the man's harangue on the need for worker solidarity against capitalists like Leibniz the Jew.

Otto had returned to his forge and was hard at work while the union boss leaned against a wagon, preaching on. Bill's patience snapped.

'Like I told the police sergeant the day I got here, I'm not interested in politics, Mister Malone. All I want is to get on with life my own way. Not be bailed up by meddling governments or organisations like yours that won't trust a man to be responsible for himself. You may as well give me up as a lost cause, I reckon.'

DRAWING·IN·PROGRESS

"THE BLACKSMITH"

THE PAINTED SWAGMAN

27

Summer mornings began in Toowoomba with a mist of fog which rolled down from the top of the Range. By nine o'clock it had dissipated, revealing streets carpeted in purple as the jacaranda trees shed their blossom. On one particular Saturday, Bill woke with a pleasant sense of anticipation; the whole town was on holiday for the annual Brewers' Picnic and he was taking the day off to join them. Otto and his family had driven off the previous day to attend a gathering at a nearby township where a renowned rabbi was visiting. They would not return until late on Sunday morning.

All the fun of a fair spread across the grassy grounds of Picnic Point with its panoramic view of the eastern Downs, dominated by the squared-off mesa called Table Top Mountain. There were concerts in the bandstand, pony rides for children, minstrel shows featuring black performers who had come out from America with Charles Hicks' original travelling shows, displays by the local dancing school and endless free beer.

Bill enjoyed it all but the sight of so many happy family groups brought on an inexpressible longing to have Tess and Billy beside him. As the day began to fade, he caught one of the omnibuses taking people back along the windswept Range road into town. At the smithy, he wrote to Tess, recounting the pleasures of the day and outlining his hopes of a secure job with Otto. At this rate, she and Billy might soon be able to join him; with luck, Tess might find a job here. That would help them to save the daunting stake they needed to start as Homesteaders and Tess had told him she was willing to try it.

When the letter was finished, Bill made a last check around the shop and its yards, propped one half of the wide front doors open for fresh air, then turned in and was soon asleep. That sleep was roughly interrupted by a second visit from d'Arcy Malone. He had come, he said, to give Bill 'one last chance to see the light'; to join in a general strike of bush workers and 'do the right thing'. Malone's message was reinforced by the fists of the bunch of bully-boys he brought with him and it took some time to deliver.

DRAWING·IN·PROGRESS

"THE BREWERS' PICNIC"

When Bill came around, it was to find the fat sergeant of police standing over him with a warning that he should be out of town by first light. Otherwise, the sergeant promised, a nasty accident might befall the blacksmith's shop; an accident which he — and his brother d'Arcy — could only regret.

Malone pulled a sulphur-tipped match from a tin box of them; rasped it to life. When the match was burning smoothly, he let it fall, flaring down to the sawdust-strewn floor. It quickly grew a ring of smouldering darkness, tiny puffs of smoke curling from it until Malone's shoe snuffed it out.

'The Union can do without your kind. So can this town. We want you out of here, Conlan.'

Bill stared in horrified fascination at the blackened ring of sawdust, remembering Otto's constant vigilance against fire. The smith had explained that more than his premises were at risk from any fire; many of his customers left their rigs for days at a time while Otto made repairs. He had asked Bill to imagine what might happen to all his tools, the very key to his livelihood, if they should go through a fire.

A little kerosene would go a long way in the smithy, Bill thought. It would be hard to prove arson. Especially with Sergeant Malone in charge of the investigation. Looking up at the brothers and their squad of toughs, Bill agreed to be gone as soon as it was light. There was little else he could do without endangering Otto. The Malones and their supporters had the town sewn up; even the storekeepers favoured a general strike.

They hoped to see the downfall of the big landholders whose business went mainly to suppliers in the cities. If the squatters could be got rid of, their land opened up to small selectors, the shopkeepers would gain a mob of new customers. Otto was hardly in the league of the squatters; but the strike was an excuse for bullying anyone unpopular. By that evening, Bill was well along the road west to Roma where, he had heard, the winery was calling for grape-pickers.

DRAWING·IN·PROGRESS

No Italians worked on Romavilla when Bill arrived there. Despite its name, the winery had been established by a Cornishman named Samuel Basset who had come up from the Hunter Valley more than thirty years before. A permanent staff lived there, performing the many delicate operations of winemaking but as the summer peaked, their numbers would swell with the influx of pickers.

It would take six weeks and more than a hundred men to clear the vines of their rich burden. The vintage was not due to start for another week but Bill walked out there anyway, hoping to find even the promise of a job when the picking began. His timing could not have been better. Weed clearing was in full swing and one of the older hands had been sent to his bed by the effects of the summer heat.

Within an hour, Bill had joined the weeding crew. At day's end, the crew gathered at Bingil Creek where they sluiced off the dust and sweat of their labours. No one undressed below the waist and no one actually entered the water above his shins. Like Bill — and like most country folk — few had ever learned to swim.

The first, lone Italian arrived on Romavilla with the picking gang in January. Girolamo Fiaschi had come out two years ago with the first group of his countrymen contracted to work the cane fields of north Queensland. With 350 others he had been recruited from a far northern province of Italy by two Italian-born businessmen from Townsville. They were under a brief from the government to find European labourers who could replace the Islander workers to whom the union movement objected.

Girolamo told Bill that all his Australian friends called him 'Gerry' and like Otto, he was multi-lingual. Besides English, he spoke French and German as well as his native Piedmontese. Soon, he was bending Bill's ear with a passionate analysis of the politics of his homeland. Gerry was extremely well-muscled and Bill could easily imagine him swinging away at the cane stalks with the hooked machete the cutters called a cane knife. Tanned to a deep mahogany, Gerry was as little troubled by the heat as any of the 'Kanakas' on the picking gang.

DRAWING·IN·PROGRESS

THE PAINTED SWAGMAN

'Kanakas' were so-called from the Polynesian word for 'man' and they originated from the many Pacific islands adjacent to Queensland. For a time, their forcible kidnapping and relocation to the cane fields made fortunes for the slave traders — European shipowners who came to be known as 'Blackbirders' — and their collaborators among the mainland businessmen in Australia and the German-held territories of the Pacific.

This disgusting trade, illegal in Britain and its colonies since 1838, began to founder after legislation passed by the Queensland government on 8 March 1868 forced each recruiting ship to carry a government official to protect the welfare of the immigrant labourers.

A push by leaders of the labour movement had forced the government to promise the end of Islander recruitment after December 1890, but since no one else really wanted the work — the same protesters having declared field labour to be 'degrading to white men' — the promise had to be temporarily withdrawn.

While uncertainty over a labour force of any kind remained, canefarmers filled the gap by replacing human workers with machines for all but the cutting of the ripe cane. Now, thousands of former cane workers were joining the search for employment. They found themselves between a rock and a hard place; with a fine irony, the union had declared 'black' any woolshed employing Aboriginal or Islander shearers or shed hands. The

infamous White Australia Policy had been born and no politician who fancied his chances at the next election dared chance his arm against its supporters.

Fruit picking was one of the few fields still open to them and on the winery, Bill was intrigued by the big, cheerful Melanesians, many of whom had brought families along. Their wives — mainly drawn from Aboriginal clans local to the sugar country — had elected to stay with them, preferring the threat of eventual deportation to their husbands' island of origin to being returned to their former tribal life. Fearing the fate which could await them, many Islanders petitioned the government for permission to stay in Queensland.

DRAWING-IN-PROGRESS

"PLANTATION"

THE PAINTED SWAGMAN

35

Islanders were not the only folk on the picking gang to be debarred by the shearers' union. Chinese were specifically excluded by the official Rules which also prescribed fines for any member who worked for, or dealt with, anyone employing a Chinese. The old Poll Tax of ten pounds for any Chinese entering Queensland had recently been lifted, only to be replaced by a thirty pound fee for permission to settle in the state. Additionally, they were now refused entry onto any goldfield until it had been open for two years, by which time the more easily won gold was usually long gone.

It all conspired to make the resented 'Celestials' feel decidedly unwelcome and they left Australia in droves. Some refused to be discouraged and they went into market gardening, merchandising, or opened eating places in the larger towns. Many stayed in the sugar towns where they had once been employed in the canefields and mills.

Here they set up emporiums to supply the still active bêche de mer industry and the predominantly Japanese diving crews of the pearling fleet which operated across the Top End. If all else failed, they led a nomadic life as fruit pickers, working on places like Romavilla, as the seasons provided. Bill found that the barriers of language and customs left him with more questions than answers about these industrious people.

With all the berries harvested and in the presses, the pickers collected their pay and dispersed to wherever they believed the next opportunity awaited. Just like the bulk of them, Bill planned to take the train for the railhead at Charleville.

There, a dozen fully-laden wool wagons had been abandoned by striking teamsters and Free labourers were needed to unload them. Police troopers and a detachment of the Mounted Infantry were on board the train, detailed to keep order at the Roll Call. Bill folded his long legs to fit the cramped space of the carriage, tipped his hat over his eyes and settled back for what he fully expected to be an uneventful journey to Charleville.

DRAWING·IN·PROGRESS

At the railhead, tent accommodations provided by the squatters were rough and ready. For many at the Roll Call, these conditions were better by far than what they had endured for the past weeks or months, tramping the country roads. Certainly, the tucker was more luxurious.

Freshly killed mutton and corned beef were laid on with lashings of black sauce; baker's bread came with cans of plum jam; and bottomless kettles of tea with both milk and sugar. At night, they dished up stews with onions and potatoes; split pea soup; sometimes a few fresh greens against the Barcoo Rot. The pastoralists knew they had to compete with the free food and tobacco on offer at the nearby strike camps.

Most of the work was unloading of the stores from the rail freight cars and lumping it to the drays which waited, rank upon rank. With hair-curling language, each bullocky directed the loading of his dray. Many carried their fearsome sixteen foot whips looped over a shoulder and looked as though they would like to use them on these unaccustomed human teams.

This convocation of bullock drivers was the largest seen in the district for some time, so many of the carriers having gone out on strike in sympathy with the rebel shearers. Now, the teamsters were feeling the pinch as the Depression and strike actions cut down the number of their customers and raised the prices of everything. Many re-examined their consciences and reckoned their union principles a poor second to feeding their families. Too much of the business they refused to handle was being taken up by Afghan camel drivers.

The turbaned drivers were becoming popular with some of the pastoralists and there were two main reasons for this. The first came down to economics: union teamsters earned four pounds in a week, while Afghans earned three pounds in a month; and this difference was reflected in their charges to the squatters. A second factor was their reliability, for as Muslims, they abstained totally from the Demon drink.

DRAWING-IN-PROGRESS

THE PAINTED SWAGMAN

The teamsters' intractability had brought a windfall for Bill and countless other men desperate for work. Though it threatened disaster for a nation in dire need of the export earnings represented by the abandoned wool clips, for Bill it meant most of twenty shillings a week that he could send home for Tess and Billy and he worked willingly while the job lasted.

Not only the Roll Call was supervised by the police and Defence Forces. Throughout the next two arduous weeks, they stood as an armed barrier between the workers and the small army of demonstrators which marched into town each day from the nearby strikers' camp.

Bruised egos and a few bloodied noses were the worst of the injuries inflicted by both sides, but the strikers' resentment had more serious consequences for the landholders of the district. Each day dawned beneath an ominous pall of smoke from grass fires. No one could prove that 'The Red Steer' had been deliberately let loose. The destruction of feed caused a havoc of frustration among the squatters and hardship for their animals.

Some of the leaders responsible for these acts were genuine in their belief in the teaching of Karl Marx, as quoted to them by union boss William Guthrie Spence:

'Only through violence can the proletariat throw off the chains of capitalism.'

Many of their followers were genuinely committed to reforms leading to what they saw as social justice. Others were nothing nobler than looters and vandals. Moderate leaders of the labour movement pleaded for restraint and some men did heed the call.

In the West, two firebrand union heroes, James 'Shearblade' Martin and Alexander Forrester, were working a different magic. Inflammatory leaflets circulated, demanding an all-out effort to 'destroy property, sheds, fences, anything that will create work' and to 'make every man join the union and thus build a fund to obtain rifles and ammunition'. To this end, the cost of the union ticket had recently doubled. Bill noticed that even the Royal Mail coach now went under armed escort.

DRAWING·IN·PROGRESS

"THE ROYAL MAIL"

THE PAINTED SWAGMAN

By the time the last bullocky had yoked his team and made a ponderous departure, the pulleys were in place to lift the top row of bales from the waiting wool wagons. Ladders were leaned against the side of each towering load and men climbed up to throw off the tie-wires as each twitch stick was loosened.

This ingenious device was used nowhere else in the world. A clever but simple use of stout saplings to tighten the tie-wires, much like a tourniquet, it had largely eliminated the risk of the enormous load shifting during its journey from the woolshed. Once down, the 250-pound bales had to be manhandled across to the rail cars for the long passage to the sea port.

As the job's end neared, some workers discovered a newfound zeal for unionism and joined the strike camp. A very few found jobs in the town but most were faced, like Bill, with hitting the Track once more. Two days outside of Charleville, he met up with a hawker's van. When he disclosed his plan of making for the next railhead at Longreach, the driver insisted that Bill ride with him. While they rattled along, Bill learned that like most of the people misnamed 'Afghan', his new friend had never seen Afghanistan.

Like Otto and others from all points of the globe, Harsha the Indian hawker had made this new land his home. Married to a woman of a Queensland tribe, he was bringing up his children to honour their Indian heritage, but to live as Australians. Bill compared this attitude with what he had learned of Gerry who was still enmeshed in the problems of the country he had fled.

He hoped that one day Gerry would, with one of those expressive Italian shrugs of his, shrug off the old feuds as well. After farewelling Harsha at Longreach, Bill did the rounds for news of a job. The only thing offering was as rouseabout on a station in the Channel Country. He lost no time in getting directions and set out as soon as he had replenished his stores. It seemed to him that the very name of the property gleamed with a message of hope: 'Golden Lakes'.

DRAWING-IN-PROGRESS

THE PAINTED SWAGMAN

April 1894, The Channel Country

On the farthest margins of the lands which can support flocks and herds — out where western Queensland meets the borders of the Northern Territory, South Australia and New South Wales — the gibber-strewn plains of the Channel Country crack and craze beneath the desert sun.

Here the ocean front of blond Mitchell grass laps against sand dunes of incandescent red. An intricate pattern of channels has been scribbled across the plains by the seasonal overflow from creeks and rivers which flow — when they do flow — into salty Lake Eyre, the relic of a prehistoric inland sea.

Rain rarely falls in any given year but during what is called The Wet, monsoon rains sweeping the far north fill dry riverbeds with flash floods. The banks overflow, spreading the plains with silver sheets of standing water. As the floods recede, lagoons called billabongs are formed and some persist for months or even years, until reclaimed by the remorseless return of drought.

While the moisture lasts, it transforms the seeming wasteland with a sudden flush of green grasses sprinkled with the multicoloured confetti of wild flowers. The secret of this periodic bonanza was cleverly exploited by Sydney Kidman — the 19th century 'Cattle King' — who started his career as a 13 year old runaway with five shillings and a one-eyed horse and ended up the largest landholder in the then British Empire.

Kidman was considered crazy when he bought up huge tracts of land out in The Overflow but as drought reduced feed on his other properties, he would shift mobs of cattle to where he knew grass would soon be available.

These drives would be carefully timed: just before the monsoonal rains made the stock routes impassable and just in time to arrive at life-giving new grass and billabongs in the Channel Country. For its human inhabitants who struggle to preserve their animals in drought times, this region is one of cyclic, crushing heartbreak. It is also, and always, a place of soaring untamed beauty. It was here that Bill found what seemed his best chance to earn a stake for Homesteading.

DRAWING-IN-PROGRESS

"THE HORSE TAILER"

Fifteen miles outside of Golden Lakes, Tom Jepson surveyed the night camp with quiet satisfaction. It had taken two hard weeks to muster the cattle from the scrub and Tom was pretty sure he'd got them all; all except a small mob of starvers that had been sighted on the far western boundary. Someone would have to go out, build up their condition before bringing them in, but they were too far out to worry about right now.

For now, Tom was happy enough to be on the home stretch. There looked to be near eight hundred in the mob bedded down here; more than a third of them cleanskins, born since the last muster. They would all have to be branded and the young bulls castrated, the store cattle cut out for droving down to the abattoirs, before what was left of the mobs could be turned loose to make for the wild country, left in peace until next mustering.

The half-wild cattle were still jumpy, agitated at being mixed in with stranger-cows and kept from breaking back to their accustomed ranges, but there had been few incidents and now he was only fifteen miles from home.

As the Boss, Tom took the first watch since he would be first up tomorrow, well before dawn, to lead the next stage. Riding slowly around the mob, Tom felt his muscles tense at the weird cry of a curlew. Any small thing might be enough to set these touchy cattle off on a rush. Apart from a few restless stirrings, the mob stayed quiet and Tom relaxed. His gravelly voice cracked out snatches of every song he knew and so awful was his rendition of these, even to his own ears, that Tom often wondered it did not send the mob rushing in self-defence.

But the cattle were no art critics. They cared little for the quality of the performance, only that it was a familiar sound, promising security from the cow-fears which prey upon cow-minds at night. Now there was movement near the centre of the ring and Tom frowned in exasperation as he spotted the baldface bull, up to its old tricks again.

D R A W I N G · I N · P R O G R E S S

THE PAINTED SWAGMAN

The old bludger had its horns under the belly of a cow, nudging her, bullying her to move so that it could lie down in the warm place she had made. If she protested too loudly, it could set off a rush. Tom was thankful when the cow just shook her head mournfully and shifted away. At the end of his watch, Tom led his mount over to the other night horses, leaving it saddled up like the rest, in case of any trouble, then sent the next man.

Trouble came on the fourth watch and no one ever knew what set it off. There came the dreaded thunder of thousands of hoofs pounding the earth; the bellowing of panicked beasts in full flight; and frantic human yells as Tom and his men fairly levitated from their swags and onto their trusted night horses.

Tom was soon on the wing of the mob, wielding his stockwhip furiously to keep the cattle from breaking back into the scrub; screaming at his men to stay between the mob and the trees; yelling for Blackburn, his best man, to take the lead and turn them.

The wild chase ended when Blackburn succeeded in getting in front, lashing the leader off its headlong path and into a circling route which brought the mob milling harmlessly in a ring. Still rolling their eyes at the stockmen, they were too tired to do more than snort and let out an occasional bewildered bellow. Tom sent a man back to bring up the wagon, for the rush had ended miles away from the night camp. He counted it lucky that

at least the stampeding beasts had headed in the general direction of Golden Lakes instead of away from it; luckier still that no one seemed to have been injured.

At the homestead, Jake Jepson had worrying news for his brother. Many of their regular shearers had written to reclaim the one pound fees they had paid to reserve a stand at Golden Lakes. Shearing was so far behind in every district that they doubted they would get to the Jepson flock this season. The brothers always hired union shearers but now Jake had been forced to advertise for Free labouring hands, just to keep things going until a shearing gang could be raised.

D R A W I N G · I N · P R O G R E S S

"TURNING THE RUSH"

THE PAINTED SWAGMAN
<u>49</u>

The following week, Tom loaded a dray with timber and provisions and drove with one of these new hands to the outstation where the mob of starvers had been spotted. He was determined to get them back to Golden Lakes as soon as they were fit for the walk. It took them a week to build a box well in the seemingly dry riverbed, with whipstick and troughs to provide water for the stranded mob. Tom found himself pleasantly surprised by the new chum, a willing worker and a good listener.

After Tom returned to the homestead, Bill missed the company and conversation more than he had expected. It was hard, hot work providing for the cattle; nearly three hundred head in poverty condition, they were a sad sight. He felt a deep satisfaction as the half-wild beasts grew to accept his presence, following him like so many dogs as he moved from one to another of the mulga trees scattered across the stony plains. At the first ring of his axe, they gathered expectantly beneath the tree he climbed, waiting for the fodder branches he cut for them.

On Tom's instructions, he spent each night half dozing beside the well, a rifle across his knees, guarding the precious water against any marauders. Tom had told him the cattle would not go near water which had been fouled by wild horses or feral pigs. Bill was glad he had not been visited by any wild boar such as Tom described: 'Four inch tusks and mad as a cut snake!' But on one unforgettable night, a mob of brumbies tried a raid on the well.

Bill held the brumby leader, a black stallion, in his sights; a perfect shot. His job was to protect the water but his hands obeyed a higher law of their own.

Raising the barrel of his borrowed Lee-Enfield, he pumped the bullets into the moon-bright sky. When it was over, only the churned-up sand around the well remained as evidence of the frantic mêlée that ensued when the enraged stallion had turned his harem to flee the two-legged enemy. In an exhilaration of spirit, Bill let go a formless yell of pure celebration, exultant at saving the water without having to kill one of the wild, beautiful creatures which had threatened it.

DRAWING·IN·PROGRESS

"AMONGST THE BRUMBIES"

THE PAINTED SWAGMAN

51

CHAPTER SIX

continued

In time, Tom returned with some of the hands and a gentle old mare on which Bill took his maiden ride. Slowly, they walked the recovered cattle back to Golden Lakes and found the homestead in a cheerful uproar: Missy Laura was home.

Half-sister to Tom and Jake, Laura had given herself permanent leave from boarding school in Brisbane. Born of their father's second marriage in his old age, Laura had been orphaned when her mother died in childbirth and the old man had soon followed her. The bachelor brothers had adopted the baby girl as their special pet and could deny their 'Princess' nothing.

Over the weeks following Laura's return, the brothers and their bemused house staff were rigorously civilised by the young Missus. Though Jake grumbled about such fripperies as napkins at mealtimes, both men smiled as they heard Laura's girlish voice singing as she planted flower seedlings or sweetly bossed the house women into more laundering than anyone but she — who did not have to do any of the work involved — considered necessary.

Inevitably, the time came when not even Laura could devise any further improvements to the homestead. For her, the hours lengthened as they grew emptier of diversions. It was just Bill Conlan's luck that the girl's attention then fixed itself on him. Bill's careful avoidance of her clumsy flirting only intensified her infatuation with him. Laura

was so accustomed to getting whatever she set her heart on, that trouble had to be the outcome when she discovered something that neither her brothers nor her own considerable charms could win for her.

Convincing herself that Bill secretly loved her and would obtain one of the new divorces if she openly declared her desire to marry him, Laura did just that; and was devastated by his startled rejection. She had made a fool of herself. There was no help for it but to banish the cause of her humiliation from Golden Lakes. Embarrassed by the situation and sorry for the unfairness of it, still the brothers were highly relieved when Bill left without making any fuss.

DRAWING-IN-PROGRESS

On the neighbouring stations, no one was looking for helpers, but it did seem they were looking out for trouble. Some homesteads had guards posted on the gates and the boundary riders were going armed. One manager let Bill stay the night, with an offer of a ride into Winton the next morning, on the cook's wagon. Even the cook drove with an old Greener twelve-bore at his side.

He explained to Bill that union rebels had staged a riot the previous week at Oondooroo station, just north of Winton. The next night, the woolshed at Ayrshire Downs had been torched. A man named Pulley had defied the rebels when they tried to burn Oondooroo woolshed; now his horse had been found in a creek, drowned and with its bridle cut to ribbons. It was a clear warning of worse trouble to come, the cook reckoned, and his hand reached down to his shotgun for reassurance.

In Winton, Bill did the usual rounds of the pubs, they being the best places to pick up news of a job. Plenty of news was flying about but it all concerned the heating up of the dispute between union bosses and the woolgrowers. The Pastoralists Association wanted to reduce rates for machine shearing but the shearers feared this was the thin edge of the wedge; accede to this and the growers would be encouraged to put machines into every shed.

Already, a squatters' group had set up a school in Brisbane where any man could learn to shear with machines in less than a week. When Bill heard about the shearing school, he only wished he had

come up through Brisbane instead of being landed at Toowoomba. That thought was one he kept to himself amongst the angry crowds.

The bitterest attacks were on a new proposal the pastoralists called Freedom of Contract. It meant that men would be free to choose not to join the union and still have equal opportunity to work any shed. Reasonable as this sounded to people like Bill, it was fiercely opposed by unionists. Tensions were running so high that a detachment of the Mounted Infantry had been billeted in Winton to back up the police who were beginning to fear the worst was still ahead of them.

DRAWING·IN·PROGRESS

Bill vividly recalled his own experience of the fight the rebels were prepared to put up; the night his train had been ambushed on the journey between Roma and Charleville. Carrying a load of Free labourers and a contingent of the Light Horse to protect them, the train was an obvious target for the rebels. Their attempt to derail it was foiled by the sharp-eyed driver. When a pitched battle ended without injury to anything but the train's green enamelled hide, a Pommie traveller, fresh out from England, expressed his astonishment at this bloodless result.

'Bullets flying everywhere; not a man scratched!' The Englishman glanced about, genuinely puzzled by what he had seen and hoping to be enlightened. All the reply he got was a few grunts, a few heads shaken in disgust at the new chum's ignorance as the men turned back to their card games or books they had been reading by lantern light.

'That "battle". A bit farcical, don't you think?' His remark proved too much for a bushman seated opposite.

'Farcical! That's how you see it? No doubt you'd have preferred a proper British battle; charge of the Light Brigade and all that? "Into the Valley of Death" and bodies lying around thick as flies.'

The man from the Bush was twice the size of the Pommie and he pushed his angry red face across the space that separated him from the flustered little man who was now shifting nervously about on the bench seat.

'Young as it is, this country's already had its "Valley of Death". We call it the Eureka Stockade and I knew men who were in it; good men.' Then he sighed.

'Never mind what the fight was about; at its end there were bodies enough to suit even you. A mixed bunch from all over, at Eureka they were united under one flag, calling themselves Australians. Opposing them, soldiers of the British Queen. Body count: twenty-two diggers, five soldiers.' Now the bushman paused, glared hard at the Englishman.

'What you saw tonight; that was Australians, facing Australians. Don't you ever forget it.'

DRAWING-IN-PROGRESS

THE PAINTED SWAGMAN

Despite being described by its admirers as a popular uprising, the Shearers' War was singularly unsuccessful in benefiting or even converting the bulk of the men on whose behalf it was supposedly fought. When standover tactics of bullying the volunteer labourers who registered for work at the Roll Calls failed, kidnapping was resorted to by radical union organisers.

The steamer 'Rodney' was ferrying volunteer workers up the Darling River to Queensland when it was ambushed by unionists near Tolarno on the night of 26 August 1894. When the fight ended, the ship was burned, the master, crew and all passengers abducted to a strike camp.

After numerous such attempts at intimidation failed to stem the flood of unemployed looking for work in Queensland, the union militants decided to carry their war to the pastoralists. During those two months of July and August, seven woolsheds were torched, grass and fences burnt and station owners and their staff attacked. But the most violent act of terrorism in this undeclared civil war was also to be the last. It occurred in the early hours of Sunday, 2 September 1894, when the defenders of Dagworth station near Winton came under siege.

The owners — Robert McPherson and his two brothers — their station-hands and two police officers were pinned down under a hail of bullets. The rebels' gunfire narrowly missed the wife and two young daughters of one of the non-union shearers sheltering in their quarters, which were well out of the line of fire to the woolshed. Most of the gunfire was cover for the unionist 'Frenchy' Hoffmeister, as he crept up to set the woolshed alight.

In the fire, one hundred and forty weaners which had been penned inside for shelter against the threatening storm, perished along with the shed. The rain came too late to save anything and washed away the tracks of the arsonists. The following day, the body of 'Frenchy' was found at a waterhole nearby, a gunshot wound to his head, a revolver in his hand. An inquest returned a verdict of suicide, so many were content to consider closed, the final chapter in a strange history.

DRAWING-IN-PROGRESS

THE PAINTED SWAGMAN

"FREEDOM FIGHTERS"

THE PAINTED SWAGMAN

59

September 1894, Winton District

When the British colonised Australia in 1788, its vast territory — only slightly smaller in land mass than the continental USA — was occupied by an ancient people, numbering around three hundred thousand, whose ancestors had migrated there some forty thousand years earlier.

Two distinct strains of people blended to form the modern Aborigines who were scattered across the continent. Remnants of a third, quite different people, were isolated from the mainland some nine thousand years before on the southern island of Tasmania.

The native Australians were one of the very few human societies never to develop agriculture or animal husbandry, although they had been made well aware of these by the Melanesian peoples who regularly crossed the Torres Strait to trade with the Australians and gather bêche de mer.

A few clans used the dingo as food, but these wild dogs were more usually kept solely for company. Fire was used as a tool to encourage the quick growth of sweet new grass, which lured a supply of game animals — wallaby, kangaroo and emu — to the waiting hunters. But systematic cultivation of crops and domestication of food or working animals remained alien to these people.

Today, some anthropologists believe this was a deliberate choice made by the original Australians whose nomadic way of life provided for their needs with relative ease. The menfolk, at least, were left with abundant free time to pursue their interest in music, song and dance; and to develop the complex and imaginative net of stories which evolved into a remarkable religious philosophy known as 'The Dreamtime'.

West of Winton, Bill was out of tucker and feeling every ounce of the weight of his swag when he happened on an elderly Songman and his family on walkabout from the sheep station which now occupied their clan's tribal grounds. The women had gathered the stems of young waterlily from the nearby lagoon and had prepared a mess of black nardoo porridge which they shared with the hungry stranger in their territory.

D R A W I N G · I N · P R O G R E S S

"BUSH TUCKER"

Impressed though he was by the generosity of the naked family, Bill found himself unable to swallow more than a token portion of the strange foods they offered him. Wistfully, he remembered the rabbiter he had met the previous day, ferrying his cargo to one of the meat-hungry strike camps. The fellow had refused to sell even one carcass to Bill.

Since the bunnies had invaded Queensland in plague proportions, government agents had begun laying poisoned baits along the frantically erected rabbit-proof fences. Now, no one dared eat rabbit unless it had been freshly shot by himself or a trusted member of his group. Bill was quite obviously not 'one of the faithful' and the rabbiter would share none of his valuable booty.

At the close of another hungry day's hike, Bill made camp beside a large waterhole where a fat ewe bent peacefully to drink. Hunger banished any thought but his need for meat and Bill soon had a sizeable chunk of that unfortunate beast roasting on his hasty fire. The rest of the mutton he shoved into his tuckerbag and hung it from a tree limb, safe from marauding meat ants.

The blackened billy was set to boil for a brew from his last handful of tea while Bill leaned back against the twisted trunk of a coolibah and savoured the comfort of a satisfied belly. He expected to reach his destination by sunset tomorrow; and now he had food enough to see that he arrived there fit and ready for work. It was some

time before he contemplated the explanations and recompense he would be required to make, when he finally reached the homestead for which he was headed.

The place for which he was making was a fair-sized sheep run called Craigielea Downs. All he knew of it was that its owners were strongly anti-union and were calling for Free labourers to man the shearing shed. When he had rolled his swag back in Winton and set out along the western road, his quest for independence had begun to seem a bit futile. Now, Bill felt buoyed with hope that its end might be coming into sight.

D R A W I N G · I N · P R O G R E S S

THE PAINTED SWAGMAN

With the early light of the next day, Bill woke to a scene of perfect serenity. On the far side of the billabong, an ethereal mist hovered above the reflections at the water's edge, drifted along the bases of grotesquely twisted coolibah trees.

All across the silvered surface, waterlilies lifted their blue heads clear of the hidden thicket of waterweeds that surrounded their stems. From some unseen clearing in the bushland, the sweeping notes of a currawong's morning song dripped through the air like music made liquid.

As Bill remained silent and still, the small life of the waterhole conducted its daily business around him. Rainbow-splashed bee eaters flitted through the branches, brilliant as jewels. Like great teardrop pearls, the cocoons of butterflies in-the-making spun from silken threads at the tips of leafy twigs.

Tiny lizards darted along the shoreline, gleaming a purple iridescence as sunlight slid over their scales. A Jesus bird picked its light-footed way over the tangle of lilypads. Dragonfly wings hummed above the golden hearts of the lilies and a fish rose to snap at them, falling back beneath the water in a tinkling splash.

In this new quietude of his mind, Bill reviewed the anxieties which had dogged every step of his journey to this point. It seemed to him that every setback and disappointment he had faced along the way had only led to some new opportunity to reach his goal. In the new certainty which suffused his thoughts, he spoke aloud the knowledge he had discovered within himself.

'There's no controlling the things that happen to us. Not really. Only how we react to what life hands us. Our attitudes to change and how we handle it. But in that, we do have total control. We always have a choice in that.'

Bill Conlan knew beyond doubt that in this land of limitless opportunity, the path he now chose would lead him to all that he truly desired.

DRAWING-IN-PROGRESS

"BILLABONG DREAMING"

CHAPTER NINE

The 21st Century, Australia

After Disraeli's Free Trade government dismantled protectionism, Britain's farmlands shrank by more than a million acres and the nation soon lost its self-sufficiency in food production. Unemployed rural workers fled into the cities and Britain restored its economy only by becoming 'Factory to the World', reliant on its colonies for raw materials and the bulk of foodstuffs. Then, as Unionism arose, British investors became nervous as many industries became less profitable; they then looked to newer countries like Australia.

With the unregulated banks and building societies of Australia falling over each other to lend out this windfall of foreign money to speculators, Sydney and Melbourne boomed. But it was borrowed money which paid for increasing imports and rapidly rising interest charges. When overseas funds dried up, due to a banking crisis which began in Argentina in 1890, the city economies expected the rural industries to bail them out of the adverse balance of payments.

As it happened, commodity prices were dropping worldwide. Silver had slumped; wheat had fallen to its lowest price in one hundred and twenty-five years; Merino wool was at its lowest price ever. It was against this scenario that the Maritime unions tied up the wharves for five months in 1890; the Miners' union cut production at Broken Hill for six months in 1892; and the Shearers' unions renewed their protracted struggle against the pastoralists in 1893.

'Wowserism' also arose at this time with many well-intentioned groups manipulating the moral and social boundaries 'for the people's own good'.

A secret labour organisation called the Knights of Labor had been formed in Philadelphia USA by Uriah Stephens in 1869. Twenty years later, it claimed one million members across the United States. In October 1890, an Australian branch was formed, attracting some of the brightest lights in the Australian push towards Socialism.

Members included Henry Lawson who became famous as the 'Poet of the People' and the English journalist William Lane who began the influential Brisbane newspaper, 'Worker'. From its pages, he agitated for extension of the eight-hour working day and his editor coined the phrase: 'Socialism in our time!'

Another effective member was G.S. Beeby who later became a Chief Judge of the Arbitration Court, ruling on disputes between unions and employers. But of these Knights of Labor, the one who was central to the orchestration of what became known as The Shearers' War was William Guthrie Spence.

After many years of organising miners' unions, Spence joined together the many small and scattered shearers' unions and was president of the Amalgamated Shearers' Union until 1893. The following year, he became general secretary of the AWU, having achieved his dream to put all bush workers under a central authority and create Australia's first super-union.

As a secret society, the Knights of Labor soon faded in Australia, for unlike the USA, it was not illegal to form or join a union here. But its legacy lived on in the American spelling adopted by the Australian Labor Party, the political arm created by the union movement.

In the century which followed the events of The Shearers' War, Australians experienced the truth of that old adage: 'The more things change, the more they stay the same'.

By the early 1980s, Australia had a Free Trade government and a de-regulated banking system, heavy reliance on foreign investment and a balance of payments debt which quickly grew into a crippling burden on a dwindling number of taxpayers. Official unemployment figures eventually topped eleven percent.

Shock ripples spreading from the stock market crash of October 1987 in New York escalated into a worldwide Recession in which Australia was among the first to suffer. Falling commodity prices and government intervention had lowered the ability of rural industries to pay the country's way out of its economic woes.

Compulsory union membership was almost universally in force and a now monolithic Council of trades unions advised the Labor federal government on many of its policies, influencing not only wages and conditions but also social welfare, foreign relations and environmental issues for the nation.

Thanks to the government's Accord with the unions' Council, strike action was mild and relatively rare during the early 1990s. That there was no real need for strike action was demonstrated by the decision handed down by a Queensland court in August 1992. A union suit against contract shearers who shore drought-stricken lambs in an effort to save their lives — and did this on a Sunday — resulted in a two thousand dollar fine against the workers involved and a goal sentence for their leader.

By early 1994, however, widespread strikes hit again in the mines and on the docks as an officially declared Recovery struggled to make itself felt by ordinary people. Well-meaning pressure groups triumphed as many and varied new rules and regulations were imposed for the 'common good', though sometimes at the expense of 'common sense'.

As the new millennium approaches, the world faces problems as dire as any in humanity's past. But an unprecedented range of technologies and philosophical tools is available to help solve them. Gloom-mongers who note only such atrocities as the on-going warfare, poverty and starvation which still afflict so many nations could take heart by remembering some of the triumphs.

Abolition of legal slavery; universal condemnation of official torture; recognition of the right of women to equal opportunity; a rising rate of global literacy; the spread of democracy and the winding-down of the threat of nuclear war between the superpowers of America and the former Soviet Union.

Despite all the fiddling of governments and pressure groups, real responsibility for their own welfare and the well-being of their society lies, always, with the people themselves. Ordinary Australians have proved to be among the most tolerant of peoples. Fanaticism never seems to get off the ground here; it is invariably countered by the Australian genius for reasonableness, by that instinct to give others 'a fair go'. In some circles, this trait is disparaged by naming it the Great Australian Apathy. Within the modern context of our strife-torn planet, it shines as a quality we might well value as our finest national asset.

WALTZING MATILDA*

Oh! There once was a swagman camped in the billabongs,
Under the shade of a Coolibah tree;
And he sang as he looked at the old billy boiling,
'Who'll come a-waltzing Matilda with me.'

Chorus:

Who'll come a-waltzing Matilda, my darling
Who'll come a-waltzing Matilda with me.
Waltzing Matilda and leading a water-bag,
Who'll come a-waltzing Matilda with me.

Chorus

Up came a jumbuck to drink at the waterhole,
Up jumped the swagman and grabbed him in glee;
And he sang as he put him away in his tucker-bag,
'You'll come a-waltzing Matilda with me.'

Chorus

Up came the squatter a-riding his thoroughbred;
Up came policemen — one, two and three.
'Whose is that jumbuck you've got in your tucker-bag?
You'll come a-waltzing Matilda with me.'

Chorus

Up sprang the swagman and jumped in the waterhole
Drowning himself by the Coolibah tree;
And his voice can be heard as it sings in the billabongs,
'Who'll come a-waltzing Matilda with me.'

* (This is the original version, as written by A.B. Paterson
on Dagworth Station near Winton, in January 1895.)

THE PAINTED SWAGMAN

69

AFTERWORD

In 1938, Paterson wrote, with tongue firmly in cheek, of his delighted surprise to be told that there really was a 'Man from Snowy River'. Dozens were claiming themselves or a relative as The Man the poet had invented. Even today, some Australians seriously debate the identity of this fictional character.

A similar compliment has been accorded The Swagman in 'Waltzing Matilda'. A few years ago, a party of sincere tourists from Marine City, Michigan USA was filmed for television as they returned to Combo waterhole on Dagworth station. Here, they had been told by their tour guide, was probably the very billabong in which the poor fellow had drowned. With some ceremony and much goodwill, they set up an engraved brass plaque to his memory and chorused 'Waltzing Matilda'.

D R A W I N G - I N - P R O G R E S S

ACKNOWLEDGEMENTS

For their help in research and modelling, the artist sincerely thanks the following persons and institutions:

Carl and Paul Wellington

Blacksmith of Sovereign Hill
Elinor East
Warren Entsch
Warren Gilbert
Marjorie and Tom Ireland
Camie McMahon
Beth, Kathy, Michael and Nathan Penhaligon
Joel Pezzutti
Bill Ryan
Lyle Squire
Teamster of Sovereign Hill
Milton Undy
Etty and Emilio Veronese
Joy and David Wall
Jared Williams

Cairns City Library
James Cook University of Townsville
National Library of Australia
State Library of Queensland
State Library of New South Wales
Qantilda Museum of Winton
Queensland Parliamentary Library
Queensland State Archives
Winton District Court (Bench Records)

FICTION: Glenkillen, Golden Lakes and Craigielea Downs are fictional places. Bill and Tess Conlan, Joseph Canning, Barney the ringer, Otto Leibniz and the brothers Malone, Gerry Fiaschi, Harsha the hawker, the Jepson family and Blackburn the drover are fictional characters.

THE ARTIST WITH HER DRAWING FOR 'BESIDE THE BILLABONG'

Dorothy Gauvin is an artist, writer and self-trained researcher of Australian history, specialising in the period of the 1890s. Born at Winton in western Queensland, she grew up in Sydney and in Toowoomba, on the Darling Downs. She now lives in Cairns with her husband and their son. Her work features in:

Queensland Parliament House (commissioned portrait)
The Castlemaine-Perkins Collection, Sydney
Private and corporate collections throughout Australia,
in Canada and the USA
Art Gallery Gauvin, CBD Cairns

Ninety-four previous oil paintings from the artist's Australia's Heritage Series have been published in book form, accompanied by writings from the nation's best-loved Bush poets. They appeared as:

"Banjo Paterson's People"
"Banjo Paterson's Australians"
"Henry Lawson's Bush Ballads"

All three titles were published by Harper Collins/Angus & Robertson Publishers in 1987, 1989 and 1991 respectively, and reached Australian Bestseller status.

In 1984, the artist spent four and a half months on a self-conducted study tour of the great galleries of Europe and returned fired with a desire to show, on canvas, all that being an Australian means to her; to share not only her love of the contrasting landscapes but the unique characteristics of the people.

The result was the start of the on-going Australia's Heritage Series and in the following year, the first group of these pictures was toured in Los Angeles, La Jolla and San Francisco where they met with enthusiastic response from Americans whose history and heritage share many features with that of Australia.

Along with her paintings on historical themes, Gauvin continues to enjoy making portraits in her 'montage' technique which tell the life story of the subject on a single canvas. Her deepest satisfaction remains the presentation, in a classical style full of drama and humour, of the colourful characters and events of our national Story.

The story of The Painted Swagman has been abstracted from a Gauvin* novel-in-progress.

* The artist's name is pronounced as 'Go — VAN'.

THE PAINTINGS

THE PAINTINGS

Each Gauvin original is crafted in permanent oil colours on finest quality Belgian linen canvas. The drawing is made directly onto the double-primed canvas with sticks of vine charcoal and acts as a grisaille to form the foundation of the painting. Sometimes this drawing is allowed to show through the underpainting in a technique the artist calls 'montaging': images which overlap each other to build an extra dimension of Time into the story depicted. Unusually for a visual artist, Gauvin begins always with the storyline, which she perfects before seeking out the people who will model the characters she has invented for the painting.

ABORIGINE: From the latin ab origine, meaning 'from the beginning', this name is given to the original or native people (and fauna and flora) of any country, especially to denote them from an invading group. In Australia, it is the most usual form of reference to those Australians descended from the people who were occupying the continent at the time of British settlement. The most accepted estimates of their numbers in 1788 vary between 251,000 and 300,000. It is calculated that the people were separated into at least 250 language groups, about 500 tribal groups being divided into numerous 'clans'.

AUSTIN Thomas: In 1859, he imported English rabbits onto Barwon Park, his property outside Geelong. By 1870, despite his having killed more than 20,000 of them, the rabbits had eaten out his property. By 1894, they had reached Queensland.

BARING BROTHERS & CO: The great financial house was founded in London by Sir Francis Baring in 1763. By 1818, the Prime Minister of France was calling it 'the sixth power in Europe'. In November 1890, the crisis caused by Argentina's default on bond payments, sent a scare through the financial world. A key partner at the time was the 62 year old Edward Baring, 1st Baron Revelstoke, who led the company out of its difficulties, meeting all obligations. The guarantors, including the Bank of England and the Banque de France, were never required to pay anything. One hundred years later, in December 1990, the merchant bank of Baring Brothers was appointed as adviser by the receiver to the failed Fairfax group of companies in Australia.

BEACH Inspectors: These officials enforced the bans on mixed and daylight swimming until the law was repealed on 2 November 1903. The ban on Sunday bathing was not lifted until 1922.

COBB & CO: Passenger and mail coach line founded in 1853 by Freeman Cobb and a group of fellow Americans. In 1856, Cobb sold his share but the company retained his name. The largest coaching firm in the country, it operated in Queensland until 1924.

COMBO WATERHOLE: Washpool on Dagworth Station where George Hamlyn Pope, a woolscourer, was discovered drowned after a night of heavy drinking on 16 September 1891.

DIVORCE: In 1894, Sir Samuel GRIFFITH, as Chief Justice, ruled in favour of a policeman who petitioned for divorce after his wife threatened to denounce him to the Labor Party as a police spy when he objected to her entertaining men at night during his absences at meetings of the Party. She carried out her threat, and as the charge was true, the man was attacked by outraged union and Labor Party members. Following his escape, he resigned from the police force and his divorce was granted.

ELDER Sir Thomas: (1818-97) Adelaide businessman who in 1866 was the first to successfully import camels into Australia. By 1890, camel strings had begun to pack loads into and from the Channel Country. In October 1894, bullocky Tom Knowles was acquitted after his trial for the murder of two 'Afghans' on the Birdsville Track, who were said to have been washing their feet in the waterhole.

EUREKA STOCKADE: Uprising by miners on the goldfields of Ballarat. Protesting an increase in prospecting fees, corruption amongst police who inspected licences, and demanding the vote for all diggers plus abolition of licences, the miners publicly burnt their licences and erected a stockade above which they flew the Southern Cross flag. Peter Lalor, their elected leader, was wounded in the ensuing battle on 3 December 1854. In 15 minutes, 5 soldiers and 22 miners were killed. Lalor escaped and remained in hiding while the other leaders were tried, and soon acquitted, on charges of treason. The following year, he was elected to parliament, becoming Commissioner for Customs, Postmaster-General and finally, Speaker of the House. In 1887, he resigned and died in 1889.

FIRST LABOUR GOVERNMENT: In December 1899, the Queensland premier resigned, advising the Governor to commission Labor member for Charters Towers, Anderson Dawson. On its first day, his government was defeated and replaced in six days. By 1894, 16 Labor members had been elected to parliament, of whom 14 were still serving.

THE FACTS

They did not include Thomas Joseph ('Tommy') Ryan, the shearer from Barcoo, who only served for one year. He is sometimes confused with Thomas Joseph Ryan, the barrister from Rockhampton who was elected in 1909 and served as Labor Premier from 1915 to 1919.

HICKS Charles: American vaudeville manager who toured Australia in the 1880s with his 'Travelling Nigger Minstrel Show'.

HOFFMEISTER Samuel: aka 'Frenchy', a union shearer born in Bavaria who was found shot to death by his own revolver, beside a waterhole near Winton on 2 September 1894.

HOWE John Robert: always called 'Jackie', shearer born at Killarney on the Darling Downs, in 1861. Despite having been a founding member of the shearers' union, Jackie Howe shore throughout the Strikes, whether the sheds were Union or black-listed, for as he explained in an open letter to the 'Western Champion' newspaper, he 'had a family to feed'. In 1900, he retired from shearing and bought the Universal Hotel in Blackall and the Barcoo Hotel in 1903. He returned to Blackall in 1907 where he lived with his wife and 8 children until 1919. In that year, he moved to 'Sumnervale', one of two pastoral properties he had purchased outside the town where he died in 1920.

LABOR: Professor Manning Clark cites 1893 as the year in which this became the accepted spelling for the Party. Certainly, by January 1893, this spelling was routinely used by the Brisbane 'Courier' newspaper, now known as the 'Courier-Mail'.

LAWSON Henry Archibald: (1867-1922) Australian-born poet and writer of short stories, activist for social reform.

LIGHT BRIGADE: Immortalised by Alfred, Lord Tennyson in his poem 'Charge of the Light Brigade', the brigade, under Lord Cardigan, suffered 40% losses in the Battle of Balaklava on 25 October 1854. Balaklava, on the Black Sea, was the supply port for the allied British, French and Turkish forces opposing the Russians during the war in the Crimea.

McPHERSON Brothers: Robert, Jack and Gideon owned and managed Dagworth station which was besieged and burnt in the early hours of 2 September 1894. All of the woolshed burnings, the attempted arson at Oondooroo, the ambush and burning of the river steamer 'Rodney' and the kidnapping of free labourers, have been reported from the official records. The revenge killing of Pulley's horse occurred two weeks after the riot on Oondooroo.

PATERSON Andrew Barton: (1864-1941) aka 'Banjo', Australia-born poet, journalist, novelist and lawyer. Visiting his then fiancee, Sarah Riley, in Winton during Christmas 1894, he was invited to visit Dagworth station. Here, in January 1895, he heard Christina McPHERSON play from memory "Bonnie Woods of Craigielea" to which he jotted down some lines of verse. The result of their collaboration is now recognised the world over as the Song of Australia.

PRIOR Charles: Committed for trial on 20 July 1894, on a charge of shooting fellow unionist Charles Ashford in the thigh during a dispute at the signing of the Roll at Coombemartin. Apart from the death of Hoffmeister, this was the only serious personal injury inflicted by either side during the Shearers' War in Queensland.

QUEENSLAND MOUNTED INFANTRY: The military unit now famous as the 2nd/14th LIGHT HORSE was formed in February 1860 when the Governor Sir George Bowen appointed Captain John Bramston as commander of the Brisbane Mounted Rifles. Various units of the Volunteer Defence Force were raised and known by their district titles. The famous emu plume decoration was, according to legend, adopted by infantrymen serving in the rural crisis of the 1890s, and officially allowed by the Queensland government after the ending the strikes. By 1915, the privilege had been extended to all regiments of the Australian Light Horse.

ROMAVILLA: The winery was established by Samuel BASSETT in 1862. His son WILLIAM, who was 8 years old in 1893, continued the winery until 1975. Since then, it has been owned and run by David and Joy Wall who have put in many improvements.

REFERENCE SOURCES

ADAM-SMITH, P. 'The Shearers', 'When We Rode The Rails'.

ALEXANDER & Williams, 'Pastoral Industries of Australia'.

ALOMES, S. 'A Nation At Last'.

Angus & Robertson, Pub. 'The A&R Concise Australian Encyclopaedia'.

ARCHER, Mrs Barbara. (Compiled) Q.S.A. Bne. 1981. 'Guide to the record of The Lands Department, 1866-1910'.

ARCHER, Thomas. 'Queensland: Her Resources and Future Prospects'.

AUSTIN, K.A. 'Cobb & Co. — The Coaching Age in Australia'. 1854-1924. Lights of Cobb & Co.

Australian Bureau of Statistics. Yearbook Australia — 1989. Queensland Yearbooks — 1983 & 1989.

Australian Meat and Livestock Corporation. 'Handbook of Australian Livestock'.

Australian Publishing Company. 'Golden Era'.

BAKER, C. 'Depressions: 1890s, 1930s'.

BARBER, George. Australia & New Zealand Encyclopaedia incl. Papua New Guinea

BEAN, C.E.W. 'On the Wool Track'.

BERNDT, R.M. & C.H. 'The World of the First Australians'. Australian Aboriginal Anthropology (ED)

BISHOP, G.C. 'Australian Winemaking, The Roseworthy Influence'.

BLAINEY, G. 'The Blainey View', 'The Causes of War', 'Gold & Paper — A History of the National Bank of Australia, 1858-1982'.

BROWNE, M. & McKernan, M. 'Two Centuries of War and Peace'.

CANNON, Michael. 'Australia — A history in Photographs', 'Life in the Cities', 'Life in the Country', 'Who's Master, Who's Man?' 'Who Killed the Koories?'

CAYLEY, Frank. 'Flag of Stars'.

CHERIKOFF, Vic & Isaacs, Jenny. 'The Bush Food Handbook'.

CHOI, C.Y. 'Chinese Migration & Settlement in Australia'.

COWAN, William C.F. 'Rollin' Yer Swag'.

CLARK, Charles Manning Hope. 'A History of Australia 1888-1915', 'A Short History of Australia', 'Select Documents in Australia's History: 1851-1900'.

CRESCIANI, Gianfranco. 'The Italians'.

COPPELL, W.G. 'Australia in Figures'.

CUFFLEY, Peter. 'Buggies & Horse-drawn Vehicles in Australia'.

Curry O'Neil Publishers. (Introduction by Geoffrey DUTTON 'Country Life in Old Australia').

DOCKER, Edward Wyberg. 'The Blackbirders'.

EDWARDS & Joyce (Editors) 'Australia — Anthony Trollope'.

ELKIN, Prof. A.P. 'The Australian Aborigines — How to Understand Them'.

FARRER, K.T.H. 'A Settlement Amply Supplied'.

FLETCHER, Marion. 'Costume in Australia, 1788-1901'.

FOX, M.J. 'History of Queensland: Its People & Industries'.

FRASER, Bryce. (Devised & Edited) 'The Macquarie Book of Events'.

GOLDSBROUGH, Mort & Co Ltd. 'Wool and the Nation'.

GROLIERS. The Australian Encyclopaedia.

HAGAN, James. 'A.C.T.U. — A Short History'.

HAMLYN, Paul (Pub.) Australia's Heritage — Vol.1

HOFFMAN, Mark (Editor) World Almanac & Book of Facts 1989.

JOHNSTON, W. Ross. 'A Documentary History of Queensland', 'The Call of the Land'.

JOYCE, Roger. 'Samuel Walker Griffith'.

LEE, Jenny & Burgmann, Verity (Editors) 'Constructing a Culture — A People's History of Australia Since 1788'.

MACINTYRE, Stuart. 'Winners & Losers — Pursuit of Social Justice in Australian History'.

MAGOFFIN, Richard. 'Waltzing Matilda — The Story Behind the Legend'.

Marshall Cavendish Ltd (Pub.) 'Times Past — Everyday Antiques in the Home'.

MATHER, Lindsay. 'Strikes & Callouts — 1st Notes of the Drum'.

Melbourne University Press. Australian Dictionary of Biography, 1891-1939.

MOORE, David & HALL, Rodney. 'Australia — Image of a Nation — 1850-1950'.

MURPHY, D.J. 'The Big Strikes. Queensland 1889-1965', 'T.J. Ryan — A Political Biography'.

MUSKETT, Dr Phillip. 'The Art of Living in Australia' (Published 1890s).

Outridge & Co (1897) 'The Work and Wealth of Queensland: Being a Sketch of the Progress and Resources of the Colony and its Daily Life'.

PALMER, Joan A. (Text) & Symes, David. (Illus.) 'The Great Days of Wool'.

POOL, S. Lane. 'Thirty Years of Colonial Government'.

POWNALL, Eve. 'Australian Pioneering Women'.

Queensland Parliamentary Library, Brisbane. Parliamentary Handbook. Queensland Criminal Code, 1899. p.147.

RAJOWSKI, Pamela. 'In the Tracks of the Camelmen'.

REYNOLDS, Henry. 'With the White People'.

SKINNER, R.E. 'Police of the Pastoral Frontier'.

SPENCE, William Guthrie 'Australia's Awakening', 'A.W.U. — 30 Years in the Life of an Australian Agitator', 'The Making of the A.W.U.'

STARR, Joan & Sweeney, Christopher. 'Forward — The History of the 2nd/14th Light Horse (Qld Mounted Infantry)'.

STONE, Derrick & Garden, Donald S. 'Squatters & Settlers'.

STONE, Walter. 'Treasury of Australian Folklore'.

STRINGER, Michael. 'Australian Horse Drawn Vehicles'.

SVENSEN, Stuart. 'The Shearer's War — The Story of the 1891 Shearers' Strike'.

TAYLOR, Peter. 'Station Life in Australia'.

TYRRELL, James R. 'Old Books, Old Friends, Old Sydney'.

VAN OUDTSHOORN, Nic (Gen. Editor) 'Front Line Dispatches — Australians at War — 1845/1972'.

WARD, Russell. 'The Australian Legend'.

WATERHOUSE, Richard. 'From Minstrel Show to Vaudeville — The Australian Popular Stage 1788-1914'.

"GREAT AUSTRALIAN HORSEMEN"

Limited Edition Fine Art Prints
by Australian artist

Gauvin

"THE TEAMSTERS"   Code DRGLO1
525mm x 665mm

"SNOWY MOUNTAINS MAN"   Code DRGLO2
630mm x 505mm

"THE DROVER"   Code DRGLO3
710mm x 505mm

"THE BRUMBY CATCHER"   Code DRGLO4
670mm x 505mm

Each print in this superb series is individually signed and numbered by the artist and has a generous white
border for ease of framing. The Edition is strictly limited to 980 Prints of each image and is produced on
finest quality acid-free stock with a subtle linen texture.

A NOTE FROM THE ARTIST

The four pictures opposite are of the first-ever release of my original artworks in the form of Limited Edition Prints. So happy was I with the meticulous care taken in their production that I sat down and wrote letters of praise to their publisher and printers.

Soon after, my own opinion as the artist was validated by the printers' peers in the industry when they won the Silver and Bronze Medals in the National Awards for Excellence in Print.

To celebrate the launching of 'The Painted Swagman', my gallery in Cairns is making the special offer on these Prints which you can share in by filling out and sending the Mail Order Form on this page.

Your purchase of the products an artist creates is the only 'applause' the artist ever hears. It is the encouragement by which any artist lives and grows; and I thank you for it.

Dorothy Gauvin

ART GALLERY GAUVIN

Conveniently located in the heart of Cairns CBD, the Art Gallery Gauvin provides a friendly atmosphere of air-conditioned ground-floor comfort backed by expert advice on the many Australian Realist artists represented. The gallery is now the exclusive outlet for all first-release Gauvin original paintings.

You will be made welcome when you visit the gallery where our aim is to present:

'Real Art of the Real Australia'

Andrejic Arcade, 55-59 Lake Street, Cairns CBD
(Opposite Orchid Plaza)
Phone & Fax 070 519403 – (A/hrs ph 070 543615)

MAIL ORDER FORM

MAIL to: FAX to:
Art Gallery Gauvin   (all hrs) 070 519403
P.O. Box 601   Ph B/hrs 070 519403
CAIRNS QLD 4870   Ph A/hrs 070 543615

Limited Edition Prints @ $ 160 each (Reg. $ 180)
Set of Four @ $ 608 Set (Reg. $ 720)

Qty	Code	Title	Price
			$
			$
			$
			$
		Set/s	$
		Please add pack and postage	$5.90
		Total	$

DELIVERY DETAILS:

Name

Delivery Address

Postcode

Phone Contact   Date   /   /

☐ Enclosed is my cheque/money order* or
☐ Please charge my credit card
☐ Bankcard ☐ Visa ☐ Mastercard

No. ☐☐☐☐☐☐☐☐☐☐☐☐☐☐☐☐

Signature   Expiry Date   /   /

* Please note: cheques and money orders should be made payable to Art Gallery Gauvin. Please allow 14 days for delivery.

GUARANTEE:

If for any reason you are not completely satisfied with your purchase, we will give you a choice of immediate replacement or refund (excluding postage and packaging.) Prints must be returned in original condition and packaging, within 30 days of receipt.